SCIENCE DETECTIVE AGENCY

Written by
STEVIE DERRICK

Illustrated by
MIRIAM SERAFIN

WAYLAND

For my beautiful girls, Matilda and Madeline,
and my wonderful husband, James - SD

For my dad, the best investigator - MS

First published in Great Britain in 2025 by Wayland
Copyright © Hodder and Stoughton, 2025
All rights reserved

Editor: Jenni Lazell
Designer: Victoria Vassiades
Consultant: Dr William H Goodwin

HB ISBN: 978 1 5263 2991 2
PB ISBN: 978 1 5263 2992 9
Ebook ISBN: 978 1 5263 2993 6

Printed and bound in Dubai

Wayland, an imprint of
Hachette Children's Group
Part of Hodder and Stoughton
Carmelite House
50 Victoria Embankment
London EC4Y 0DZ

An Hachette UK Company
www.hachette.co.uk
www.hachettechildrens.co.uk

The authorised representative in the EEA
is Hachette Ireland, 8 Castlecourt Centre,
Dublin 15, D15 XTP3, Ireland (email: info@hbgi.ie)

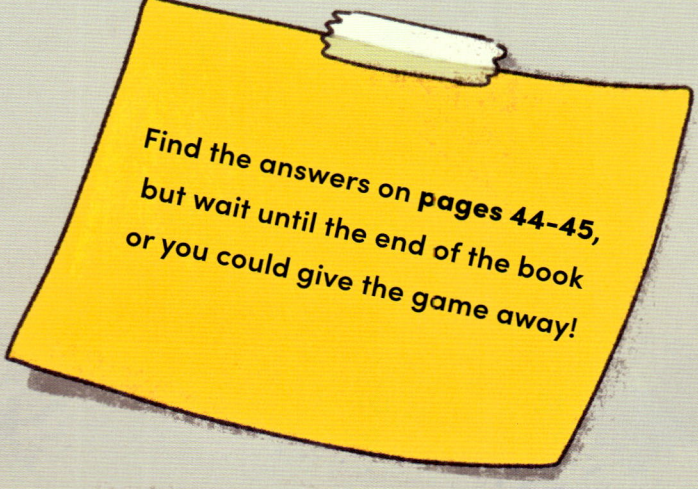

Find the answers on **pages 44-45**, but wait until the end of the book or you could give the game away!

CONTENTS

4-5 Become a science detective

6-7 Science fights crime

8-9 There's been a crime!

10-11 Crime scene investigation kit

12-13 The crime scene

14-15 Witness statements

16-17 Check the suspects

18-19 Collecting fingerprints

20-21 Leaving prints

22-23 Soil samples

24-25 Examine fragments

26-27 Spatter patterns

28-29 DNA detectives

30-31 Let's go digital

32-33 Robots at the ready

34-35 Eye spy

36-37 Hairy business

38-39 Bite marks

40-41 Who dunnit?

42 Quiz

43 Meet a forensic scientist

44-45 Answers

46 Glossary

47 Find out more

48 Index

Maddie

BECOME A SCIENCE DETECTIVE

Welcome to the Science Detective Agency. Here, we solve crimes and catch criminals. If you're here, it's because you have the sharp eye and snappy brain that's needed. It's time to train you up, but first, let's find out what a science detective actually is.

Science detectives are also called forensic scientists or crime scene investigators (CSI). Using their science smarts, they collect evidence that can help catch criminals. Here are a few examples of what forensic scientists can collect from a crime scene.

FINGERPRINTS

Fingerprints are unique to each individual, even identical twins. The ridges of prints are formed on human babies when they are still growing in the womb!

DNA

DNA is like a recipe book for how your body works and functions. Scientists can look at DNA from a crime scene to identify a single person.

FIBRES

Tiny fibres can fall off a criminal's clothes when they're rushing about or get snagged on a broken window.

DIGITAL EVIDENCE

Whenever you look at a website, you leave a record on your laptop or phone. Digital forensic scientists can search the laptop to find out whose login details were used.

BUGS

Mouldy bread with maggots on it might look gross, but it can tell scientists a lot about when a crime was committed. It takes time for maggots to hatch from eggs laid in bread left out.

PLANTS AND FUNGI

Soil samples left at crime scenes can contain fungi or pollen. These can show scientists where a criminal has been and even what time of year the crime was committed.

SUPER SLEUTH SEARCH

Forensic scientists need to be really good at looking for evidence. It's time to test your observation skills. Look at these two pictures of a crime scene, before and after the crime was committed. Use your powers of observation to spot 10 differences between these pictures.

Read the rest of the book before you check out your answers on page 44.

SCIENCE FIGHTS CRIME

Forensic scientists piece together clues from crime scenes to solve cases. Today, these clues can be DNA from hair or blood, fingerprints, or tiny fibres from the criminal's clothes, but hundreds of years ago, it wasn't so easy to solve a crime. Despite the lack of modern technology, science has been busting criminals as far back as the 2nd century CE.

TIMELINE

44 BCE
When Roman leader Julius Caesar was killed, doctors wanted to find out which of the 23 knife wounds killed him. So, they performed the first autopsy, which is a medical examination of a body.

1890
Francis Galton was the first person to figure out how to measure fingerprint patterns. The first criminal convicted because of his fingerprints was the burglar Harry Jackson, who left his prints on a freshly painted windowsill and was sent to prison in 1902.

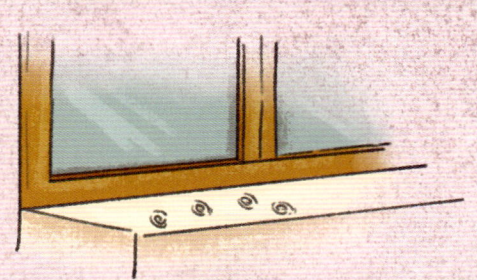

2001
Ötzi the Iceman is a 5,300-year-old mummy found perfectly preserved in ice in 1991. Scientists performed a CT scan (a special scan that looks at the inside of your body) on Ötzi in 2001 and discovered that he had died from being shot by an arrow. One of the oldest ever cold cases was finally solved.

2020s
The 21st century has seen a boom in robotics and AI (artificial intelligence). AI can help scientists search through thousands of DNA samples, sift through hours of video footage, and help find faces in a crowd using facial recognition technology, much faster than human detectives.

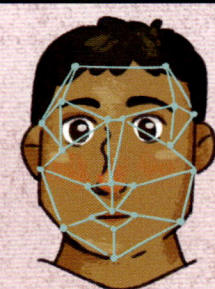

75 CE
A blind man was accused of killing his father with a sword in Ancient Rome. The criminal left bloody handprints all along the wall of the crime scene. After inspection, the man's lawyer found the handprints were from the stepmother and not the son.

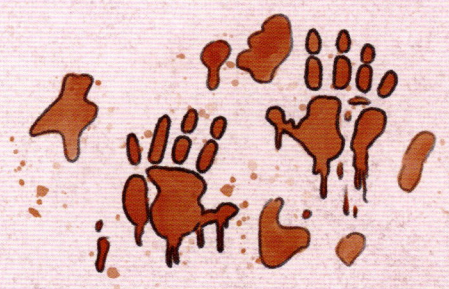

1784
Detectives were searching for a murderer in Lancashire, UK. A piece of newspaper was found on the murder weapon. After a tip-off, detectives searched a man called John Toms. They found a similar piece of newspaper in his pocket. The two pieces of paper were a perfect match and Toms was convicted of the crime. This was the first time someone had been convicted using physical evidence.

1901
Before the 1900s, it wasn't known that people had different blood types – type A, B, O, and AB. Karl Landsteiner made this discovery in 1901 and almost immediately it was used to help scientists catch criminals by matching their blood types to samples found at crime scenes.

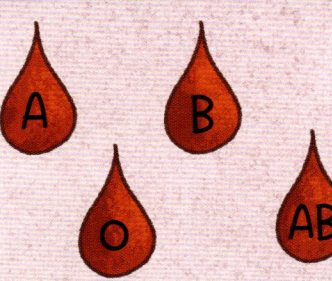

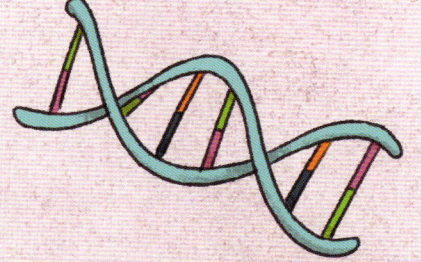

1984
Sir Alec Jeffreys discovered DNA profiling, which identifies the part of your DNA that is completely unique to you. DNA profiling was first used to prove someone's innocence and catch the real criminal in 1986.

Wow, forensic science has changed so much in 2,000 years! But wait, science detective, it looks like we have a real crime to investigate.

THERE'S BEEN A CRIME!

Crime report number: 02062020
Date: 10 July
Time: 17:10

Incident details: A call came in at exactly seventeen hundred hours (5pm). The victim? Twelve-year-old Maddie Michaels. She claims that someone has used her streaming account to watch a film, without her permission! The rented film wasn't included in her subscription, so she has been charged extra. She has no idea who watched the film, so she needs the help of the Science Detective Agency.

Maddie has given us a timeline of her day.
Do you think you can spot when the crime might have taken place?

MADDIE'S DAY

7:00 — Maddie wakes up and has toast for breakfast. She watches TV and plays with her little brother, Jamie and big sister Matilda.

9:00 — Maddie's mum takes her and her siblings to their swimming lesson. Her dad and granny have gone shopping. The house is locked up.

10:30 — Swimming lessons end so they go out for a hot chocolate and play in the park before heading home.

12:00 — Everyone comes home to have lunch together. Sandwiches and apple slices. Yum!

14:00 — Maddie gets a call from some of her friends. They are playing in the local park and want her to join. She heads out, leaving everyone else at home.

17:00 — She comes home to find broken glass – and that a crime has been committed. She immediately calls the Science Detective Agency.

> You will need your super sleuth skills and best science work to solve this case. Do you think you have what it takes?

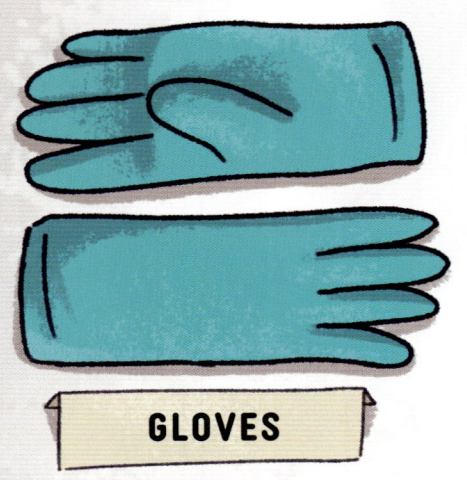

GLOVES

It's important that CSIs don't leave any of their fingerprints at the scene. Gloves will help protect you when you're collecting evidence.

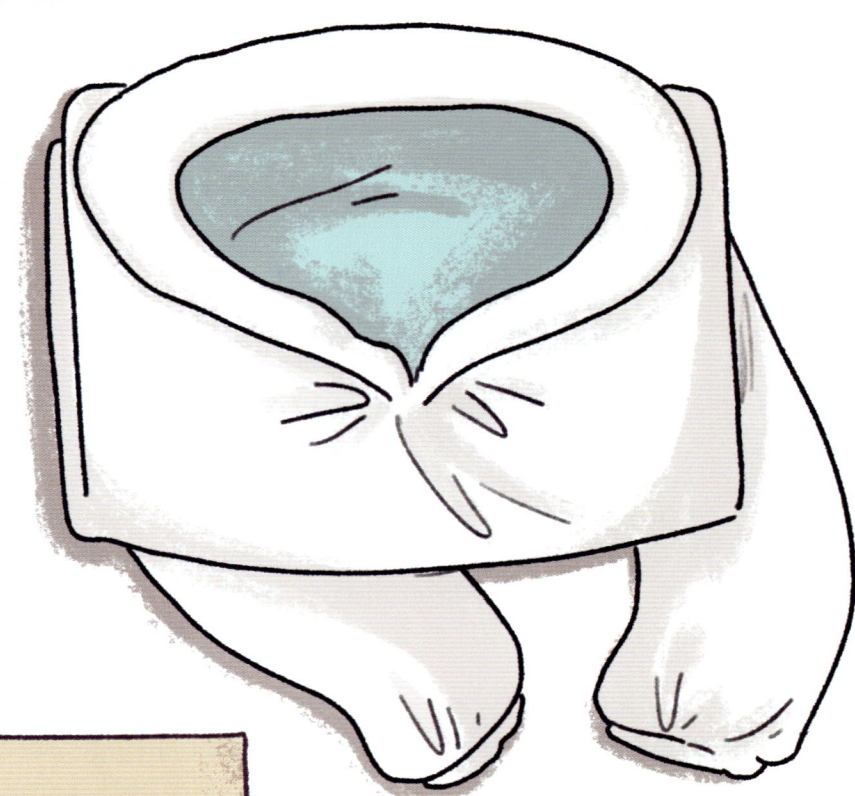

CRIME SCENE INVESTIGATION KIT

It's time to grab your tools and head to the crime scene. But first, let's see what you've got in your kit. Forensic scientists need lots of special equipment so they can collect evidence without contaminating the scene.

CLEAN SUIT

You can't shed fibres or hair if you're wearing this suit.

CRIME SCENE TAPE

This lets everyone know that there has been a crime and stops people from entering the scene.

NOTEPAD AND PEN

Taking notes is important when you're collecting crucial evidence.

CAMERA

Photographs help detectives look over all of the evidence at once to see if they can spot any clues as to who committed the crime.

EVIDENCE BAGS

All of the evidence collected needs to be put away safely in these bags so it can be sent to the lab for further testing.

MAGNIFYING GLASS

Get a closer look at evidence with this handy gadget.

FINGERPRINT BRUSH AND POWDER

Collecting fingerprints could help you catch the criminal.

CRIME SCENE MARKERS

Every piece of evidence needs to be documented. These markers make sure you haven't forgotten anything.

Now you've got everything, let's head to the crime scene to see what evidence has been left behind.

WITNESS STATEMENTS

Interviewing witnesses is an important part of an investigation. It helps paint a picture of what happened before and after the crime took place. Witnesses can often forget details or remember them differently, so don't take what everyone says as the absolute truth.

WHAT WE KNOW

Based on Maddie's timeline of events, we know that the crime took place somewhere between 14:00 and 17:00 – that's a three-hour window. Let's see what everyone was up to during that time.

Dad – 'I was in the garden looking after the plants.'

Granny – 'I was asleep all afternoon.'

Mum – 'I was in the office working on the computer.'

Neighbours – 'We were playing football in the front garden and accidentally kicked the ball through the window. We are sorry!'

Jamie – 'I was outside playing football with the neighbours.'

Matilda – 'I was in my room doing my homework at that time.'

STATEMENTS

Well, that explains the mysterious ball and the broken window, but it doesn't mean they didn't watch a film afterwards. It looks like they are all suspects until we have more information.

Look at page 16-17 to get a clearer picture of where everyone was.

THE SCIENCE

When you remember something, tiny connections form in the brain between your brain cells, or neurons. These connections are called synapses and they help rewire your brain.

The more you are exposed to an activity, like lessons for playing a musical instrument, the more connections are created and the better you are at remembering that activity. The less exposure, however, the weaker those connections become, and you may forget that activity.

Memories are stored in the hippocampus.

TEST YOUR MEMORY

Witnesses may be able to remember some things, but it is harder to remember the details. For example, they might remember the colour of the house where a crime was committed, but they probably won't remember how many windows it had.

Let's test your memory. Take a look at these **10 objects** for **10 seconds**. Try and remember as many as you can. Now, cover them up and write down as many of the objects as you can remember.

- Your remembered five objects – your memory is pretty good.
- You remembered seven objects – that's some pretty great remembering.
- You remembered all 10 objects – whoa, do you have super memory?

CHECK THE SUSPECTS

Now we have our list of suspects, we need to look at the bigger picture. Take a look at the blueprint, or floorplan, of the house to see where everyone was. We can check their alibis against this.

WHAT WE KNOW
We have everyone's witness statements. Everyone says they weren't anywhere near the living room when the crime took place.

Mum says she was in the study, but the study is right next to the living room. Was she telling the truth?

GROUND FLOOR

GRANNY'S FLAT

Dad says he was in the garden. There was no one else around. It will be hard to check his alibi.

Jamie and neighbours kicked the ball through the window. How did they not see someone sitting in the living room?

THE SCIENCE

An alibi is where someone says they were somewhere else when the crime was committed. A really good alibi would be if a suspect were with a large group of people far way – they could all confirm the suspect was nowhere near the crime. Or, if a picture was taken of a suspect somewhere else, proving they couldn't have been the culprit.

Granny has never used a streaming site before so she can easily be ruled out.

Matilda says she was in her room the whole time, doing homework. There isn't any sign of homework, but her phone is still warm. Was she messaging a friend, instead?

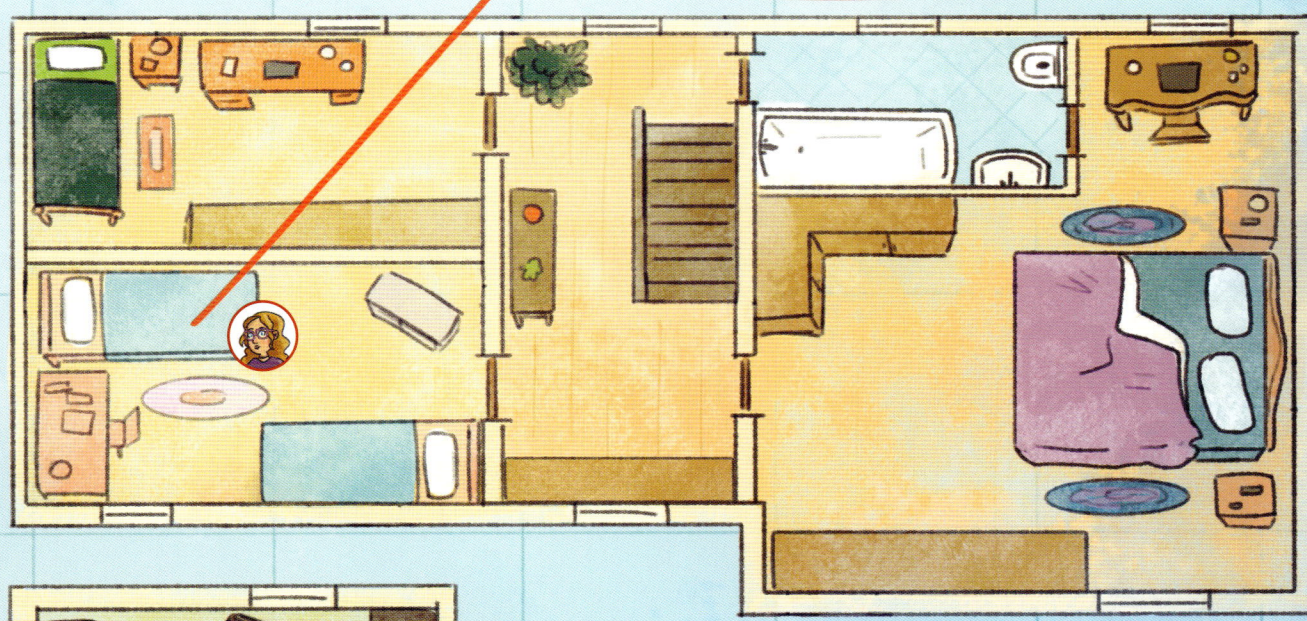

FIRST FLOOR

GRANNY'S FLAT

You've checked the alibis and found out that mum went upstairs to take a nap between 3-4pm and wasn't working the whole time – the bed does look crumpled, so she's probably telling the truth. Matilda confirms she was listening to music, messaging her friends and didn't actually do her homework. Granny has been ruled out.

Well done for revealing the truth, but we are no closer to finding the real culprit. Maybe checking fingerprints will help.

COLLECTING FINGERPRINTS

'Every contact leaves a trace.' Those are the watchwords of forensic scientists. One of those traces is fingerprints. Let's check for those.

WHAT WE KNOW

The only way to play the film is to use the remote control. That means the culprit may have left their fingerprints on it. However, there will also be fingerprints from everyone who uses the television.

THE SCIENCE

The fingertips and the palms of the human hand are soft and flexible and covered in tiny ridges. These ridges help the skin to grip objects. Everyone has a unique pattern of looping and twisting ridges on their fingertips. The skin is kept soft by oils, and some of the oils are left behind when the finger touches something. The oils keep the pattern of the skin ridges, and we call this a fingerprint.

Forensic scientists compare the prints they find at a crime scene with samples collected from the suspects. These are the three main types of fingerprints.

Arch　　Loop　　Whorl

THE TEST

A crime scene investigator generally 'dusts' for fingerprints. They sprinkle very fine white (aluminium) powder over the surface. Some of the dust will stick to the oily print. The rest will brush away. The investigator can then press tape onto the dusty print to make a copy of it. For really faint fingerprints, investigators have a neat trick. They sprinkle a special dust that makes fingerprints glow under an ultraviolet light, turning them red, yellow and orange.

FIND A MATCH

These are the fingerprints from the remote control, can you match them to the fingerprints collected from the suspects?

THE RESULTS

Well done! The remote control is covered in fingerprints. You've found the thumbprints of every suspect that lives in the house, but not any belonging to the neighbours (but someone could've helped them watch the film). It seems like there is a mysterious unknown print as well.

LEAVING PRINTS

Like fingerprints, footprints are also unique. Every person's foot has a special set of ridges that can identify them. However, not many criminals walk around barefoot, so scientists can also work out who committed a crime from their shoe print.

WHAT WE KNOW

Muddy footprints leading from the kitchen all the way to the living room were found at the crime scene. Let's test them and find out who they belong to.

THE SCIENCE

Scientists will study a footprint by uploading it to a computer and seeing if there are any matches to other crime scenes. The size of the print also allows scientists to work out roughly how tall a criminal is, and a deep footprint will give scientists an indication of the weight of the person. All of these things can help investigators figure out who committed the crime.

THE TEST
It's been a busy day at the Michaels' household. People have been running through the kitchen with muddy feet. Can you match the footprints to the shoes? Go back to page 8 to look at the suspects' footwear.

Here's the footprint lifted from the crime scene. What shoes do you think made these tracks?

THE RESULTS
It looks like the culprit was wearing slippers, but there are a few people in this house who wear slippers and they could have changed their shoes. We've since learned Jamie is the only person who doesn't regularly wear slippers. Can we rule him out?

SOIL SAMPLES

If a footprint at a crime scene contains traces of soil, then crime scene investigators can study this soil to see where it came from. The idea of using soil to catch criminals is called forensic ecology.

THE SCIENCE
Here are a few things forensic ecologists can gather:

Soil
Soil is a mixture of rocks, minerals, living organisms and water and air. It can also contain pollen from plants, insects or animal droppings. By looking at the soil, scientists can work out where a culprit has been.

WHAT WE KNOW
A muddy footprint was found at the crime scene. The culprit must have walked through the garden, but where exactly in the garden did it come from? Let's find out.

Insects
Bugs like to eat dead animal and plant matter. By looking at what types of bugs are eating the rotting material, investigators can get an exact time of when the crime was committed.

Tiny organisms
Bacteria and fungi are microorganisms – these are life forms so small they can only be seen under a microscope. When you leave food out, bacteria or fungi start to grow on the food. By looking at this growth, scientists can work out how long the food has been there.

THE TEST
Investigators look at the soil from the muddy footprint through a microscope and match this to other soil samples from around the garden. They have also found an insect in the soil. It is a small scabious mining bee. These bees only like one type of plant. Investigators can match the bee to the plant in the garden.

FOLLOW THE POLLINATOR
This is a picture of the Michaels' garden. There are lots of different types of plant. Can you work out which plant the small scabious mining bee came from?

RESULTS
Well done! You've worked out that the soil came from the part of the garden next to the granny flat.

EXAMINE FRAGMENTS

At a crime scene, forensic scientists can collect fragments of physical evidence that can be used to paint a picture of how a crime was committed. Fragments might include hair, fibres or a piece of glass. Let's see what fragments we have collected.

Window

WHAT WE KNOW
There were two types of glass found at the crime scene. The window was smashed with the neighbours' ball, but where did the other glass come from?

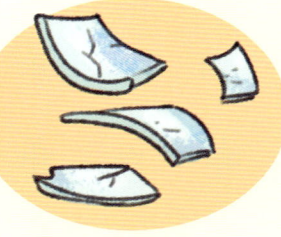
??

THE SCIENCE
Glass is basically sand heated to extreme temperatures – about 1,700°C. The way the sand is heated and the chemicals that are added create a unique glass structure, which forensic scientists can compare against other pieces of glass.

THE TEST
Investigators first need to check whether they have all the pieces of glass. When a glass jar is dropped, shards of glass can travel up to 4.5 m in any direction.

When they have collected all of this evidence, they look at it under a microscope to check if the pieces match any at the crime scene.

As well as working out where the glass came from, investigators look at the distribution of the glass (where it landed) and figure out at what height it was dropped or if it was smashed by a hard object, like a baseball bat.

FIX THE GLASS

Match the mystery shards of glass to similar objects on the right. What clues do you see in the different glass shapes to tell you what object it might have been?

 **a)** Broken window

 **b)** Broken mirror

 **c)** Broken jam jar

 **d)** Broken glass

THE RESULTS

Great work, science detective. It looks like the shards of glass comes from a jam jar. One must've been dropped!

SPATTER PATTERNS

Forensic scientists can study spatters to see how and where a liquid was dropped. This liquid could be blood, paint or even jam. Let's see how these spatter patterns help catch the criminal.

WHAT WE KNOW
When the jam jar was dropped the sticky jam splashed everywhere!

THE TEST
Forensic scientists will look at the spatter patterns to try and work out the angle and the height the jam jar was dropped from. They may even do a few tests in their lab to see if they can recreate the spatters themselves.

EGG DROP!
Try this experiment at home (with your grown-up's permission!) to see how spatters look from different heights.

You will need:
- 6 different colours of water-soluble paint
- 6 eggs in an egg carton
- Outside space
- Overalls
- Goggles
- White paper

1) Ask a grown up to crack the top of six eggs then clean them out of all the egg. Use the leftover egg to make omelettes. Yum!

2) Fill each eggshell with a different coloured paint.

3) Set up your outside space with lots of white paper. Wear some overalls or old clothes and pop on some goggles.

(4) Drop your paint-filled eggs from different heights to see how the spatters look different (you may want to ask an adult to use a ladder for the last one). Use new sheets of white paper for each test. What do you see?

If you drop something from a low height, it doesn't have far to reach the ground, so doesn't break with as much force. If something is dropped from a greater height, gravity has more time to speed it up, making it hit the ground with more force, so the eggs that are dropped from a greater height should have larger spatter patterns.

THE RESULTS

The jam was dropped by someone with a height of around 150 cm. Here are the heights of all the suspects. Can you rule anyone out?

Mum is 163 cm

Dad is 180 cm

Matilda is 152 cm

Jamie is 120 cm

Neighbours are 120 cm

It's time to test the DNA and see if it matches up with the DNA from any of the suspects.

DNA DETECTIVES

DNA, or deoxyribonucleic acid, is the blueprint for all life on Earth. It can be found in every cell in your body. If a criminal leaves some hair or skin cells at a crime scene, the DNA in the cells can be tested to find out who that criminal is.

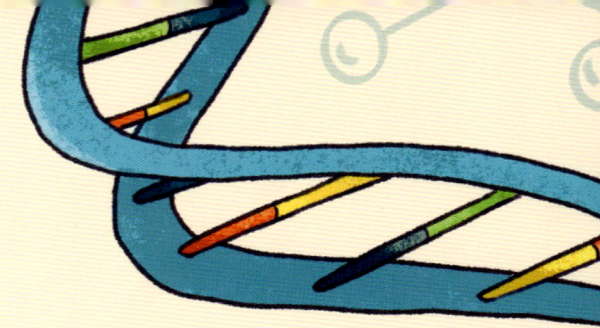

WHAT WE KNOW

We've swabbed the mug and found some saliva on it. Let's head to the lab so we can test the DNA.

THE SCIENCE

DNA looks like a twisted ladder. This is called a double helix. Every human on the planet shares 99.9% of the same DNA. The differences – and what makes you, you – are contained in just 0.1% of DNA. Forensic scientists can test this small amount to find out who the culprit is, or someone who the culprit might be biologically related to. This is because you share some of the same DNA with your parents and siblings.

THE TEST

Forensic scientists need to transport any DNA samples to a laboratory in a cool bag or refrigerator. At the lab, the DNA is removed from the sample and replicated, which means more and more is created. This gives scientists enough DNA to check it against their system to see if there are any matches. If they can't find any direct matches, they will look for relatives, too.

MATCH THE DNA

Take a look at your witnesses' DNA and find the closest genetic match to the DNA from the mug. This will tell you if the suspect is related to anyone.

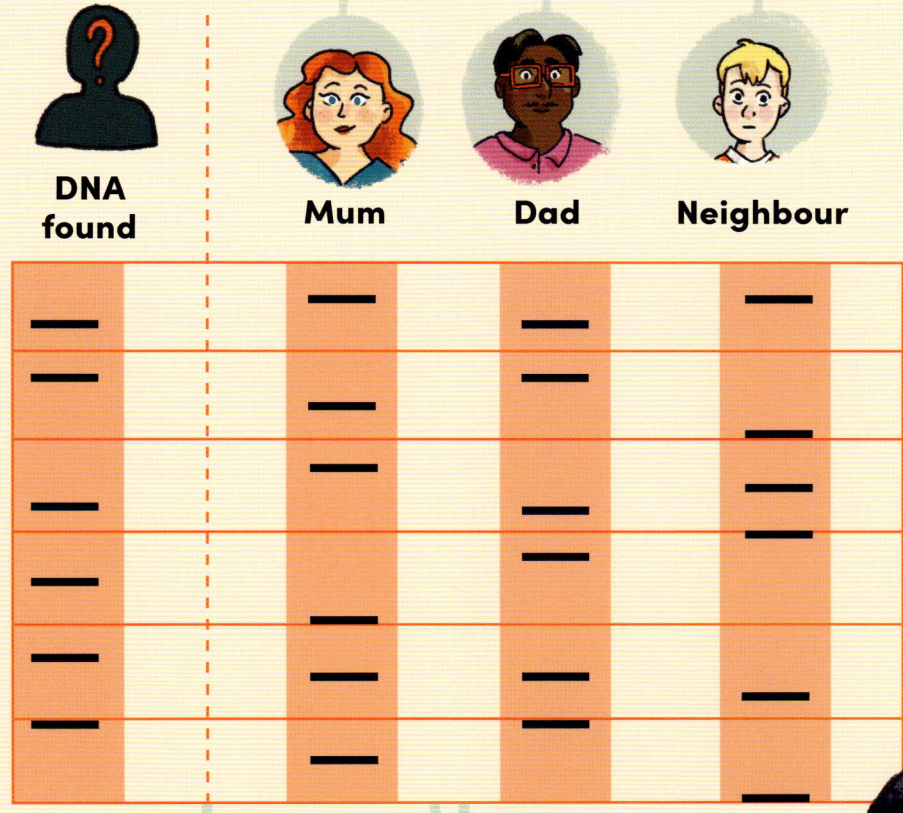

THE RESULTS

Wow, great detective work! It looks like some of the genetic markers are a match to dad – this means he is related to the culprit. That rules out mum and the neighbours.

LET'S GO DIGITAL

Digital forensics is the process of collecting and analysing digital data – this is any data on an electrical device, such as a phone or laptop. The smart TV was used to access the film – let's find out who used it.

WHAT WE KNOW

A film was watched between 3 and 5pm on a smart TV. The culprit downloaded the film from Maddie's streaming account. A password is needed to access this account.

THE SCIENCE

All the information that is stored on a digital device is stored the same way. Information, such as files, text and images, are stored as 1s and 0s. This is known as binary code. It is the most basic form of computer code.

Computers store information in their memory, but they can also store it in the Cloud. Cloud memory is stored on servers in huge data centres located all over the world.

Streaming films works in a similar way. When you log onto your account and select a film to watch, the streaming platform can detect where you are, and it sends the film across the internet from the nearest data centre. All of this happens in seconds.

THE TEST

Forensic scientists can access any electronic device. From the device, they can uncover hidden data, such as deleted search history, documents and any films watched. Digital detectives might run a piece of software to uncover any secrets from the streaming platform, such as who logged on to watch the film and the exact time the film was watched. The software converts the data from computer language (binary code) into data that investigators can read.

CRACK THE CODE

The exact time the film was watched is hidden behind this code. Use the key to solve the puzzle then check which clock shows the correct time.

6 18 13 14 14
6 7 14 1 6 25
20 26 17 14

2	4	9	3	14	20	24	18	26	5	21	10	15
A	B	C	D	E	F	G	H	I	J	K	L	M

1	16	19	8	13	22	6	12	17	7	23	25	11
N	O	P	Q	R	S	T	U	V	W	X	Y	Z

THE RESULTS

Well done, you've cracked the code! Now we know what time the film was watched. Mum was sleeping from 3-4pm and Maddie's brother was playing football.

ROBOTS AT THE READY

Artificial intelligence (AI) is the ability of a computer system to 'think' and perform tasks that usually require human intelligence. AI is being used more and more in forensic science to help sift through vast amounts of data quickly, helping pull files in record time and catch criminals quickly and reliably.

THE SCIENCE

AI robots use a process called deep learning to find a fingerprint match. Deep learning is a technique that teaches computers how to detect similarities between two sets of fingerprints by getting trained with photos.

For example, to train an AI system to recognise photos of a cat, millions of photos are uploaded into the machine. The photos are labelled 'cat' or 'not a cat'. The system then picks out important features from the images labelled 'cat'. Eventually, the AI would be able to tell you if an image contained a cat or not, even if it wasn't labelled.

WHAT WE KNOW
There was a mysterious print found at the crime scene. Running this fingerprint through AI software could help get a match in the system.

Deep learning goes one step further. If it makes a mistake, it can rewrite its own programming to fix that mistake so that it doesn't make it again – learning similar to a human brain.

THE RESULTS
The software has been running in the background and it found a match to a suspect who forgot to pay for parking 20 years ago. There's an image to go with the fingerprint match, but it is hard to make out. Can you work out the culprit from this blurry image?

EYE SPY

Your eyes are incredible! The only other organ more complex than the eye is the brain. Glasses can help fix people's vision, but if they are found at a crime scene then they can also be used to catch the criminal.

Vitreous - clear gel that fills the eye

Retina - light-sensitive layer that sends signals through the optic nerve to the brain

WHAT WE KNOW
A pair of glasses was found at the scene. Before we test who they belong to, we need to learn more about how the human eye works.

THE SCIENCE

When you see something, light travels through your eye to the retina (a light-sensitive layer of tissue at the back of the eye). Cells in the retina called photoreceptors turn the light into electric signals. These electric signals travel through the optic nerve to your brain. Your brain then processes these signals as images. Most people who wear glasses do so because the light travelling through the eye doesn't focus on the retina properly, causing blurry vision.

Optic nerve - nerves that carry signals from the retina to the brain

THE TEST

Forensic scientists can check glasses prescriptions. However, many people have the same prescription so this may be hard to identify a person.

In 1924, a man called Nathan Leopold was convicted of murder after a pair of glasses fell out of his pocket at the crime scene. Even though the prescription was common, his glasses had a special part that was only made by one company and only three other people had those same glasses. Leopold was found out and convicted of the murder.

Sclera - the white outer coating of the eye

TEST YOUR EYESIGHT

Stand 3 m away and look at this chart. What is the lowest line you can see clearly? 20/20 vision means you have very good vision. If you can only read the letters above this line, you may need glasses.

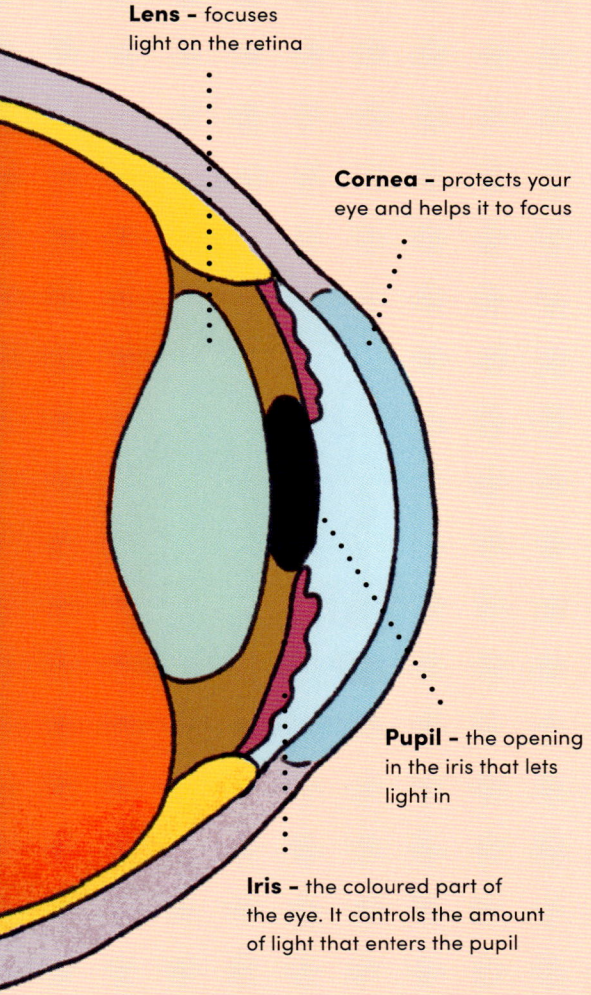

Lens – focuses light on the retina

Cornea – protects your eye and helps it to focus

Pupil – the opening in the iris that lets light in

Iris – the coloured part of the eye. It controls the amount of light that enters the pupil

THE RESULTS

The glasses found on the floor could belong to three people in the house, who all need glasses to help them see and have similar prescriptions – Dad, Jamie and Matilda. Did someone else drop their glasses?

E	1	20 / 200
F P	2	20 / 100
T O Z	3	20 / 70
L P E D	4	20 / 50
P E C F D	5	20 / 40
E D F C Z P	6	20 / 30
F E L O P Z D	7	20 / 25
D E F P O T E C	8	20 / 20
L E P O D F C T	9	20 / 15
F D P L T C E O	10	20 / 13
P E T O L C F Z D	11	20 / 10

35

HAIRY BUSINESS

If you're lucky, the culprit has left some hair at the crime scene. Hair is a very important tool for forensic scientists and can tell investigators a lot about what a culprit may look like.

WHAT WE KNOW
Hair was found on the couch at the scene of the crime. Did this belong to the culprit, or does everyone who sits on the couch leave hair evidence behind?

THE SCIENCE

Your hair colour is determined by your DNA and a pigment (a natural colouring) called melanin. If your hair has a lot of melanin, you have dark brown hair. If you have much less, you have blonde hair. Red hair is caused by a pigment called pheomelanin. As you age, your hair colour might change. When we get older, the hair follicles – structures within your skin that grow your hair – stop being able to produce melanin, so your hair turns grey.

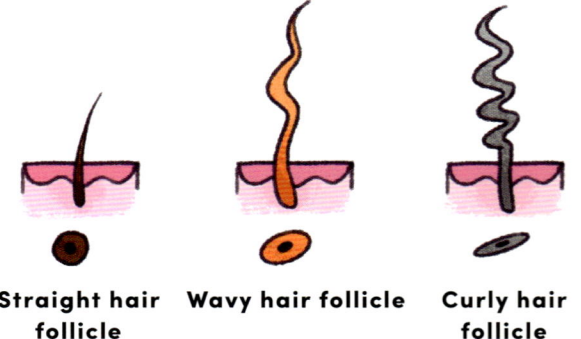

Straight hair follicle   **Wavy hair follicle**   **Curly hair follicle**

STAGES OF HAIR GROWTH

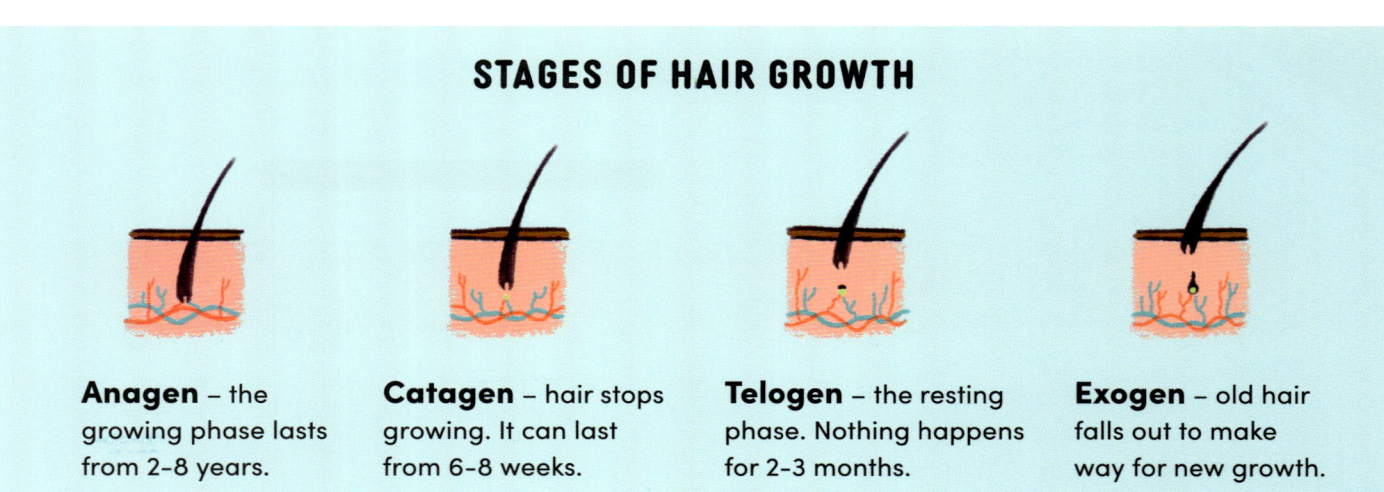

Anagen – the growing phase lasts from 2–8 years.

Catagen – hair stops growing. It can last from 6–8 weeks.

Telogen – the resting phase. Nothing happens for 2–3 months.

Exogen – old hair falls out to make way for new growth.

THE TEST

Investigators can look at hair under a microscope. If the hair still has a follicle, it may contain DNA, which can be tested. If not, there is still a lot scientists can tell from the hair sample, such as what colour hair the culprit may have and whether or not the hair has been dyed.

Sometimes people curl or straighten their hair, so the best bet is to look at the follicle to tell what hair type they have (straight or curly). If the hair follicle has an oval shape, it means the culprit has curly hair. If the follicle is round, then their hair is straight.

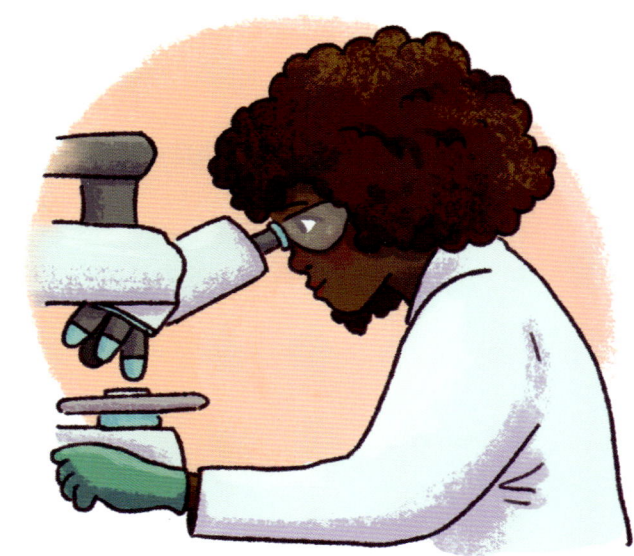

MATCH THE HAIR TO THE SUSPECT

Look at the couch from the crime scene – there's a lot of hair on it. Can you match the hair to the suspect?

Mum

Matilda

Jamie

THE RESULTS

It looks like a lot of people sit on this couch, but some grey hairs were also found. Very suspicious.

BITE MARKS

All humans have a unique tooth structure – which means that people can be identified from their teeth and their bite marks. Forensic scientists can check these and match them against dentists' records.

WHAT WE KNOW
An apple core was found on the floor. With a tooth stuck in it!

Enamel · · · Dentine · · · Pulp · · ·

Gums · · ·

Root canal · · ·

THE SCIENCE
When children are little, they have baby teeth – 10 on the top and 10 on the bottom. Kids typically start to lose these at about the age of six as adult teeth come through. Adults have 32 teeth: incisors, canines, premolars, molars and wisdom teeth (although some people cannot see their wisdom teeth as they get stuck in their gums.)

The structure of your teeth looks like this.

THE TEST
First, forensic dentists test the tooth that was stuck in the apple and see if it matches any of the suspects. When you get older, your teeth might fall out and false teeth will be put in. False teeth are made from plastic or metal.

PROTECT YOUR TEETH

Try this activity at home to see how different liquids can damage your teeth. Eggs work really well because the shells contain calcium, which is also found in your teeth.

You will need:
- 3 eggs
- 3 jars
- Dark fizzy drink
- Vinegar
- Water

1. Fill one jar with fizzy drink, one jar with vinegar and one jar with water.

2. Pop an egg in each jar and cover for three days.

Fizzy drink   **Vinegar**   **Water**

3. On the fourth day, take the eggs out of the jar and see the differences.

The sugars in the fizzy drink have stained the egg. The vinegar has caused the shell to dissolve completely, while the water hasn't damaged the egg at all. Any drinks other than water can damage our teeth. You must make sure you brush your teeth twice a day for two full minutes each time to protect them.

THE RESULTS

Scientists back at the lab have tested the tooth and found that it is made from a type of plastic called acrylic. It looks like whoever ate this apple had false teeth.

I think we have enough to go on. Let's check through all of the evidence and see if we can catch the culprit.

39

WHO DUNNIT?

That's some amazing science detective work. We have so much evidence to go on. Let's put it all together and see if we can work out who the culprit is.

FINGERPRINTS

There were fingerprints from everyone in the house, but also a mystery fingerprint. No fingerprints of the **neighbours**.

DNA

The DNA taken from the mug of tea showed that the culprit was a relative of **dad**. That ruled out **mum** and the **neighbours**.

FOOTPRINT

The culprit wore slippers. **Jamie** is the only person who doesn't wear slippers.

SOIL SAMPLES

Tests showed that the offender walked through the garden at some point, getting mud all over their slippers.

QUIZ

1. What is a medical examination on a body also called?

2. What type of fingerprint is this?

3. Which two things can investigators find out from a footprint?
a) height
b) eye colour
c) weight

4. At what distance can glass travel when it has been broken?
a) up to 1.5 m
b) up to 3 m
c) up to 4.5 m

5. True or false? Investigators can collect pollen from soil samples to find the culprit.

6. What is deoxyribonucleic acid also known as?

7. What is gravity?

8. Anagen is the stage where your hair falls out. True or false?

9. What numbers represent binary code?

10. How many adult teeth do humans have?
a) 53
b) 46
c) 32

MEET A FORENSIC SCIENTIST
Meet Keith Elliott, a forensic scientist and DNA expert

What does a forensic scientist do?
A forensic scientist carefully studies the evidence in a case using scientific techniques to help investigators and those involved in the legal courts (judges, jurors, lawyers) understand exactly what happened.

How did you become a forensic scientist?
I was interested in the world from a young age. When I was nine, I loved hunting for bugs in the garden and reading science fiction stories. I studied biology at university and then did a Masters degree in forensic science. I wrote to EVERY police force in the UK to ask if I could shadow crime scene examiners for a day and was lucky enough to get the chance to do this a couple of times. I got a job in a forensic lab (just collecting the samples as they came in from the police and 'booking them in'). I was then more easily able to find out about jobs coming up and eventually got a job creating new forensic methods.

Can you give an example of how forensic science is being used today?
A friend of mine, Ray Wickenheiser, once recovered DNA from part of a contact lens found in a vacuum cleaner bag at the crime scene. The DNA was actually from the victim, who didn't report the crime until days later, so there wasn't a lot of other evidence at the crime scene. The DNA found on the contact lens was able to prove her story was true and eventually convict the real criminal, who admitted to the crime before the trial.

What's the future of forensic science?
I think over the coming years we'll see forensics helping more in investigations where there are no suspects – helping to give investigators more leads. This will involve things like predicting the physical appearance of suspects, and even using DNA to tell investigators who to look out for on CCTV images.

What advice would you give to a child who would like to study forensic science?
Most forensic science labs are not looking for young scientists with forensic degrees. They want good general science knowledge. They can teach you the forensic science as long as they see the solid understanding of science. Look out for any summer schools in forensic science, study hard at school and take an interest in science.

ANSWERS

PAGE 4-5

PAGE 8-9

The crime took place between 14:00 and 17:00.

PAGE 18-19

Fingerprint 1 - Jamie
Fingerprint 2 - Mum
Fingerprint 3 - Matilda
Fingerprint 4 - Dad

PAGE 20-21

The footprints were made by slippers. (But the culprit could have changed their shoes ...)

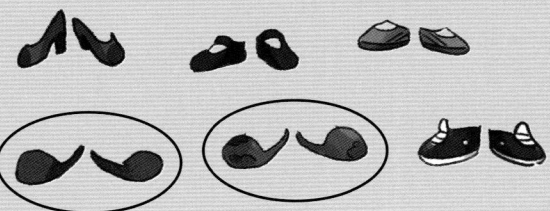

PAGE 22-23

The small scabious mining bee matches with the Devil's-bit scabious plant in the garden.

PAGE 24-25

c) Broken jam jar

PAGE 28-29

The suspect's DNA is the closest match to Dad.

PAGE 30-31

Three twenty-five

PAGE 32-33

This looks the most like Granny might have 20 years ago.

PAGE 36-37

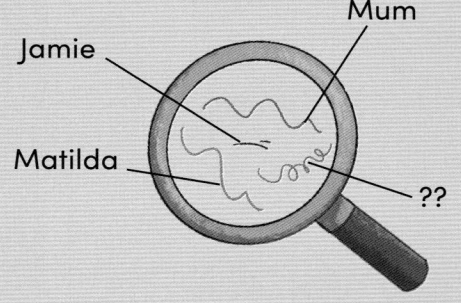

QUIZ ANSWERS (PAGE 42)

1. Autopsy
2. An arch fingerprint
3. a) height c) weight
4. c) up to 4.5 m
5. True
6. DNA
7. The invisible force that keeps your feet on the ground
8. False, it is called exogen when your hair falls out
9. 1 and 0 represent binary code
10. c) 32

THE RESULTS!

The culprit was **GRANNY** all along! You should never rule out a suspect too early. Check all of the evidence first. Granny says the film was great and the whole family should watch it.

Some great investigating, science detective!

Remember, to be a science detective all you need to do is be curious, have a sharp eye and take an interest in science. Great work!

SOLVED

GLOSSARY

Alibi
A statement by a person under suspicion of a crime, saying that they were in a different place at the time.

Artificial intelligence
A smart machine that is able to 'think' for itself and perform tasks that usually require human intelligence. These include problem-solving, decision-making, learning and reasoning.

Autopsy
A medical examination of a body to find out how a person died.

Cold case
A crime that has never been solved.

Computer programming
Instructions that computers can follow to perform tasks.

Contaminate
To leave something behind at the scene that shouldn't be there.

CT Scan
A test that takes images of the inside of your body.

Culprit
A person who is responsible for a crime.

Data centre
Huge buildings where lots of digital information is stored.

DNA
A complex chemical found in every cell that tells your body how to grow and develop. Its full name is deoxyribonucleic acid.

Ecology
The study of every living thing in every environment.

Evidence
Anything that can help prove that something is or is not true.

Hippocampus
A part of the brain that helps with learning and memory.

Spatter patterns
The pattern of stains made when a liquid hits a surface.

Suspect
Someone who the police think broke the law.

Victim
Someone who has been harmed as the result of a crime.

Witness
Someone who saw a crime taking place.

Womb
Where an unborn baby develops and grows.

FIND OUT MORE

Check out these books and websites to become an expert on forensic science and the human body.

Read What is DNA? (Wayland 2024) by Professor Julian Barwell and Dr Neeta Lakhani to learn more about your body's blueprint.

Read Kay's Anatomy: A Complete (and Completely Disgusting) Guide to the Human Body (Penguin 2021) to learn more about the human body.

Meet a forensic expert that uses clues at crime scenes to help solve cases with Operation Ouch!
www.youtube.com/watch?v=4u-pdQvAp3A

Who messed up the classroom? Help solve a case with Science Trek.
www.youtube.com/watch?v=PJlplQpPl6E

Put your crime-solving skills to the test in this murder mystery game.
exploring-mars.le.ac.uk/story.html

Become a forensic science expert with this handy guide.
www.twinkl.co.uk/teaching-wiki/forensic-science-for-kids

We strongly advise that Internet access is supervised by a responsible adult. The website addresses (URLs) included in this book were valid at the time of going to press. However, it is possible that contents or addresses may have changed since the publication of this book. No responsibility for any such changes can be accepted by either the author or the Publisher.

INDEX

A
alibis 16, 17
artificial intelligence 6, 32, 42

B
bacteria 22
binary code 30, 31
blood 7, 12, 26
brain 15, 34, 35

C
computer 14, 20, 30, 31, 32
crime scene 4, 5, 6, 7, 10–11, 12–13, 20, 22, 24, 28, 34, 36, 37, 43
criminal 4, 5, 6, 7, 11, 20, 22, 26, 28, 32, 34, 43
CT scan 6
culprit 12, 13, 17, 18, 21, 22, 28, 29, 30, 33, 36, 37, 39, 40, 41, 45

D
deep learning 32
digital forensics 4, 30–31
DNA 4, 7, 27, 28–29, 35, 40, 42, 43, 44

E
evidence 4, 7, 10, 11, 12, 24, 36, 39, 40, 43, 45
eyes 34–35

F
facial recognition 6
fibres 4, 10, 41
fingerprints 4, 10, 11, 18–19, 32, 33, 40, 42, 44
follicles 36–37
footprints 12, 20–21, 40, 42
Francis Galton 6
fungi 5, 22

G
glass 13, 24, 25, 42
glasses 13, 34, 35, 41
gravity 27

H
hair 36–37, 41, 42, 44
hippocampus 15

I
insects and bugs 5, 22–23

J
John Toms 7
Julius Caesar 6

K
Karl Landsteiner 7

M
melanin 36
microscope 22, 23, 24, 37

N
neurons 15

O
Ötzi the iceman 6

P
plants 5, 22–23

S
Sir Alec Jeffreys 7
software 32, 33
soil 5, 22, 23, 40
spatters 26–27
suspects 16, 18, 19, 27, 29, 33, 37, 38, 45
synapses 15

T
teeth 38–39, 41, 42

W
witnesses 13, 14–15, 16